T0057084

Bob Chilcott
Anthems 2

8 anthems for mixed voices

MUSIC DEPARTMENT

OXFORD
UNIVERSITY PRESS

OXFORD
UNIVERSITY PRESS

Great Clarendon Street, Oxford OX2 6DP, England
198 Madison Avenue, New York, NY 10016, USA

Oxford University Press is a department of the University of Oxford.
It furthers the University's aim of excellence in research, scholarship,
and education by publishing worldwide in

Oxford New York
Auckland Cape Town Hong Kong Karachi
Kuala Lumpur Madrid Melbourne Mexico City Nairobi
New Delhi Shanghai Taipei Toronto

With offices in

Argentina Austria Brazil Chile Czech Republic France Greece
Guatemala Hungary Italy Japan Poland Portugal Singapore
South Korea Switzerland Thailand Turkey Ukraine Vietnam

Oxford is a registered trade mark of Oxford University Press
in the UK and in certain other countries

© Oxford University Press 2009

Bob Chilcott has asserted his right under the Copyright, Designs
and Patents Act, 1988, to be identified as the Composer of these Works

Database right Oxford University Press (maker)

First published 2009

All rights reserved. No part of this publication may be reproduced,
stored in a retrieval system, or transmitted, in any form or by any means,
without the prior permission in writing of Oxford University Press,
or as expressly permitted by law. Enquiries concerning reproduction
outside the scope of the above should be sent to the Music Copyright
Department, Oxford University Press, at the address above

Permission to perform the works in this anthology in public
(except in the course of divine worship) should normally be obtained
from the Performing Right Society Ltd. (PRS), 29/33 Berners Street,
London W1T 3AB, or its affiliated Societies in each country throughout
the world, unless the owner or the occupier of the premises
being used holds a licence from the Society

Permission to make a recording must be obtained in advance
from the Mechanical-Copyright Protection Society Ltd. (MCPS),
Elgar House, 41 Streatham High Road, London SW16 1ER,
or its affiliated Societies in each country throughout the world

10

ISBN 978-0-19-336493-6

Music and text origination by
Enigma Music Production Services, Amersham, Bucks.
Printed in Great Britain on acid-free paper by
Caligraving Ltd, Thetford, Norfolk.

Contents

A Thanksgiving	4
Dear Lord and Father of mankind	15
Love divine	27
Queen of the May	37
Let the earth acclaim him	44
The Lord's my Shepherd	46
The Lord's Prayer	53
This day	59

Composer's note

These eight pieces have been written over the past three years, and all but two are in print for the first time. Both 'The Lord's my Shepherd' and 'This day' were previously published with alternative scorings, and I have prepared new SATB versions for this collection.

I grew up singing the daily service of Evensong, first as a chorister and choral scholar in the Choir of King's College, Cambridge, and later as a temporary lay clerk in the Choir of Westminster Abbey and a freelance singer in many of the beautiful churches in London. It offered on a daily basis a time of reflection and quiet within the walls of some great buildings and spaces. The resonance of this aspect of my musical life has never gone away, and has deeply influenced my work as a composer, particularly in this collection of recent anthems.

I would like to thank Philip Croydon, Jane Griffiths, and Robyn Elton for their work on this publication.

Generously commissioned by Jerry & Cathie Fischer, Ken & Penny Fischer, and Jack & Linda Hoeschler for The King's Singers in celebration of their 40th Anniversary

A Thanksgiving

St Richard of Chichester
(*c.*1197–1253)

BOB CHILCOTT

*This anthem is for unaccompanied double choir, but may also be performed by Choir 1 only, with organ accompaniment.

First performed by The King's Singers and the Choir of King's College, Cambridge, at King's College Chapel, on 1 May 2008.

© Oxford University Press 2009. Photocopying this copyright material is ILLEGAL.

5
mp espress.
for all the be-ne-fits which thou hast giv-en us,
div. mp espress.
thanks be to thee, for all the be-ne-fits which thou hast giv-en us,
mp espress.
thanks be to thee, for all the be-ne-fits giv-en us,
mp espress.
for all the be-ne-fits giv-en us,
thanks, thanks,
thanks, thanks,
thee, to thee,

9
p
for all the pains and in - sults which thou hast borne for us.
p
for all the pains and in - sults which thou hast borne for us.
p
for all the pains and in - sults which thou hast borne for us.
p
for all the pains and in - sults which thou hast borne for us.
mp
thanks to
mp
thanks be to
mp
thanks
mp

12
p
thee, thanks be to thee, to thee, to thee.
div.
p
thee, to thee, to thee, to thee, to thee, thanks.
p
thanks,
be to thee, to thee, to thee, to thee, thanks, thanks be to
p

16
unis. mp
O most mer-ci-ful re - deem-er, re-deem-er, friend, and
mp
O most mer-ci-ful re - deem-er, re-deem-er, friend, and
p
Thanks, thanks,
p
Thanks, thanks,
p
unis.
thee, thanks to thee, to
div. p
Thanks, thanks,
Ped.

19
mf
may we know thee more clear - ly, love thee more dear - ly,
mf
div.
bro - ther, may we know thee more clear - ly, love thee more dear - ly,
mf
bro - ther, may we know thee more clear - ly, love thee more dear - ly,
mf
may we know thee more clear - ly, love thee more dear - ly,
mp
thanks, thanks,
mp
thanks, thanks,
mp
thee, thanks, thanks,
mp
thanks, thanks,
mp

22
mp cresc.
f
— and fol-low thee more near-ly, day by day, may we
mp cresc.
f
— and fol-low thee more near-ly, day by day, may we
mp cresc.
f
— and fol-low thee more near-ly, day by day, may we
mp cresc.
f
— and fol-low thee more near-ly, day by day, may we
mp
may— we
mp
may— we
mp
may— we
mp
may— we
mp

25
mp
know thee more clear - ly, love thee more dear - ly, and
mp
know thee more clear - ly, love thee more dear - ly, and
mp
know thee more clear - ly, love thee more dear - ly, and
mp
know thee more clear - ly, love thee more dear - ly, and
mf
know thee, love thee.
mf
unis.
know thee, love thee.
mf
div.
know thee, love thee.
mf
know thee, love thee.
mf

28
fol - low thee more near - ly, day by day.
fol - low thee more near - ly, day by day.
fol - low thee more near - ly, day by day.
fol - low thee more near - ly, day by day.
mp
Thanks to
mp
Thanks be to
mp
Thanks
mp
Man.

30
thee, thanks be to thee, to thee, to thee.
div.
thee, to thee, to thee, to thee, to
be to thee, to thee, to thee, to

32
rit.
p
A - - men.
unis. p
A - - men.
p
A - - men.
p
A - - men.
p
A - - men.
unis. p
thee, thanks. A - - men.
p
thee, thanks. A - - men.
p
A - - men.
rit.
p
Ped.

Commissioned to celebrate the 450th Anniversary of the foundation of Repton School

Dear Lord and Father of mankind

J. G. Whittier (1807–92)

BOB CHILCOTT

The optional congregation part that enters at bar 71 is the standard hymn tune 'Repton' by C. Hubert H. Parry (1848–1918).

First performed in Repton School Chapel on 26 May 2007, directed by John Bowley.

© Oxford University Press 2009. Photocopying this copyright material is ILLEGAL.

9
fool - ish
of man - kind, For - give our fool - ish,
13
ways!
poco cresc.
fool - ish ways! Re - clothe us in our
poco cresc.
poco cresc.
17
f
right - ful mind, In pu - rer lives thy
f
f

21
mp
ser - vice find, In deep - er, deep - er
mp
mp
25
p
re - verence praise.
p
p
29
T.
B.
unis. mp
In sim - ple trust like theirs who heard, Be - side the
mp

33
S.
A.
T.
B.
unis. mf
mf
The gra - cious call - ing of the
Sy - rian sea,
mf
36
S.
A.
Lord, Let us, like them, with - out a word Rise up and
39
f
fol - low thee, rise up and fol - low thee.
f
f
dim.

43
p
O Sab-bath rest by Ga - li-lee! O
T.
p
B.
p
(Man.)
48
mp espress.
calm of hills a - bove, Where Je - sus knelt to
mp espress.
mp espress.
(Ped.)
52
unis.
share with thee The si - lence of e - ter - ni-ty, In -
unis.

56
- ter - pret-ed by love, in - ter - pret-ed by
60
p
p espress.
love!
Drop
p
p espress.
p

*If not sung by the congregation, this part should be performed by a small group of singers from the main choir.

72
mf
cease.
Dear Lord and
from our souls the strain and stress,
Lord and Fa - ther of man-kind, For - give our fool - ish ways! Re -
76
f
Fa - ther, dear Lord, Dear Lord and Fa-ther,
And let our or - dered lives con - fess
- clothe us in our right - ful mind, In pu - rer lives thy ser - vice find, In

80
mp
p
For - give, for - give our fool - ish ways!
mp
p
The beau - ty, beau - ty of thy peace.
mp
p
mp
p
deep - er re - verence praise, in deep - er re - verence praise.
mp
p
84

88
S.
A.
p
Breathe through the heats of our de - sire
T.
B.
T.
p
B.
p
(Man.)
92
mf
Thy cool - ness and thy balm; Let sense be dumb, let
mf
mf
(Ped.)

96
flesh re - tire; Speak through the earth - quake, wind, and fire,
99
DESCANT
mp
Drop thy still dews of qui - et - ness,
S.
A.
mp
p
O still small voice of calm, O
T.
B.
mp
p
mp

102
p
drop thy still dews of
still small voice of calm, O still small voice
p
105
rit.
pp
qui - et - ness.
pp
of calm!
pp
rit.
pp

to Terry and Alyce Price; given with love and deep appreciation for them both on the occasion of their tenth year in service at Preston Hollow Presbyterian Church, Dallas, TX; and for the profound gift of their many decades of service to Christ and to His Church

Love divine

Charles Wesley (1707–88)

BOB CHILCOTT

© Oxford University Press 2009. Photocopying this copyright material is ILLEGAL.

7
S.
A.
T.
B.
unis.
mp dolce
Fix in us Thy hum - ble dwell - ing, All Thy
10
cresc.
Je - su,
T.
B.
faith - ful mer - cies crown.
cresc.
cresc.
Ped.
13
Thou art all com - pas - sion, Pure, un - bound - ed love Thou

16
f
art; Vi - sit us with Thy sal - va - tion, En - ter
f
f
19
dim.
mf dim.
ev - ery trem - bling heart, en - ter ev - ery trem -
dim.
mf dim.
dim.
mf dim.
22
poco rit.
a tempo
mp
- bling heart. Come, Al -
mp
poco rit.
a tempo
mp
Man.

25
S.
A.
Come, Al - might - y to de - li - ver, all Thy
T.
- might - y to de - li - ver, Let us all Thy life re -
B.
- might - y to de - li - ver, Let us all Thy life re -
Ped.
28
life re - ceive; Sud - den - ly re - turn, and
- ceive, all Thy life re - ceive; Sud - den -
- ceive, all Thy life re - ceive;

31
ne - ver, ne - ver more Thy tem - ples leave.
- ly re - turn, and ne - ver more Thy tem - ples leave.
Sud - den - ly re - turn, ne - ver more Thy tem - ples leave.
34
mf
Thee we would be al - ways bless - ing, Serve Thee
mf
Thee we would be al - ways bless - ing, Serve Thee
mf
Thee we would be al - ways bless - ing, Serve Thee
mf

37
S.
A.
T.
B.
f
as Thy hosts a - bove, Pray, and praise Thee, with - out
40
ceas - ing, Glo - ry in Thy per - fect love, glo - ry
43
poco dim.
mf
in Thy per - fect love.
unis.
Fin-ish

47
T.
B.
then Thy new cre - a - tion, Pure and spot - less let us
50
unis. mf
S.
A.
Let us see Thy great sal - va - tion, Per - fect -
T.
B.
be;
53
cresc.
S.
A.
f
- ly re - stored in Thee. Changed from glo - ry in - to
f
cresc.
f

56
glo - ry, Till in heaven we take our place, Till we
59
ff
cast our crowns be - fore Thee, Lost in won-der, love, and
ff
ff
62
dim.
f dim.
A.
praise, lost in won-der, love, and
dim.
f dim.
dim.
f dim.

65
rit.
a little slower
S.
mp
praise,
lost in won - der,
mp
rit.
a little slower
68
poco rit.
Tempo I
p
love,
and
praise!
p
unis.
Love di -
poco rit.
Tempo I
p dolce
Man.
72
unis.
Love di - vine, all loves ex - cel - ling, love di -
- vine, all loves ex - cel - ling, love di - vine, all loves ex -

75
- vine, all loves ex - cel - ling, Joy of
- cel - ling,
78
S.
A.
heaven, to earth come down.
T.
B.
Ped.
81
rit.
rit.
pp
Man.

for the marriage of Jonna and Quinn

Queen of the May

Trad. 19th cent.

BOB CHILCOTT

*The percussion part may be played on any appropriate instrument, e.g. handbells, crotales, chime bars, or triangles.

© Oxford University Press 2009. Photocopying this copyright material is ILLEGAL.

23
blos - soms to - day, O Queen of the An - gels and Queen of the
28
f
S.1
May. O Ma - ry, we crown thee with blos-soms to - day, O
S.2
A.
May. O Ma - ry, we crown thee with blos-soms to - day, O
T.
B.
33
Queen of the An - gels and Queen of the May.
Queen of the An - gels and Queen of the May.

38
unis.
T.
B.
Their la - dy they name thee, Their mis - tress pro-
43
- claim thee. O, grant that thy child - ren on earth be as
47
true; As long as the bow - ers Are ra - diant with
51
flow - ers, As long as the a - zure shall keep its bright
55
S.
A.
O Ma - ry, we crown thee with blos - soms to -
T.
B.
hue.

59
day, O Queen of the An - gels and Queen of the
63
S.1
May. O Ma - ry, we crown thee with blos-soms to - day, O
S.2
A.
May. O Ma - ry, we crown thee with blos-soms to - day, O
T.
B.
68
Queen of the An - gels and Queen of the May.
Queen of the An - gels and Queen of the May.

74
S.1
Sing gai - ly in cho - rus, The bright an - gels o'er us Re - e - cho the
S.2
A.
Sing gai - ly in cho - rus, The bright an - gels o'er us Re - e - cho the
T.
Sing gai - ly in cho - rus, The bright an - gels o'er us Re - e - cho the
B.
Sing gai - ly in cho - rus, The bright an -
80
strains we be - gin u - pon earth; For Ma - ry, for Ma - ry,
strains we be - gin u - pon earth; Their harps are re - peat - ing The notes of our
strains we be - gin u - pon earth; Their harps are re - peat - ing The notes of our
- gels o'er us. For Ma - ry her - self is

86
— for— Ma - ry— is the cause of our mirth. O
greet - ing, For Ma - ry her - self— is the cause of our mirth. O
greet - ing, For Ma - ry her - self— is the cause of our mirth. O
— the— cause of— our— mirth.— O
91
S.
A.
Ma - ry, we crown thee with blos - soms to - day, O
T.
B.
95
ff
Queen of the An - gels and Queen of the May. O
ff
ff

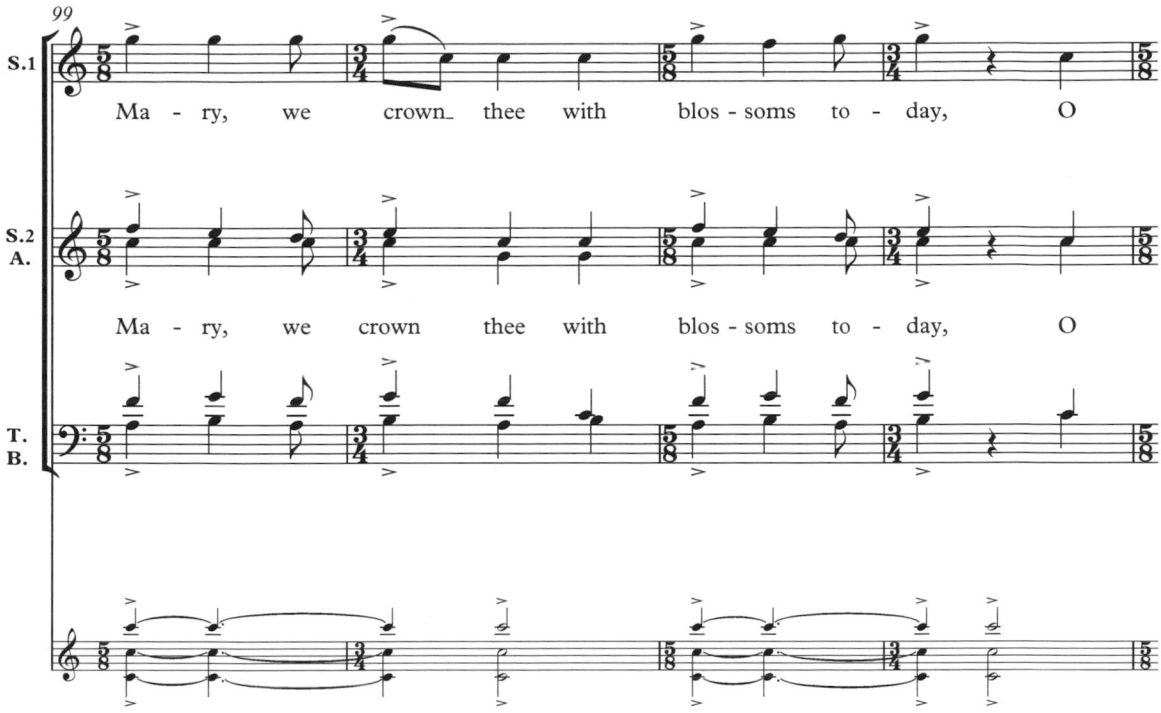
99
S.1
Ma - ry, we crown thee with blos - soms to - day, O
S.2
A.
Ma - ry, we crown thee with blos - soms to - day, O
T.
B.

103
Queen of the An - gels and Queen of the May.
Queen of the An - gels and Queen of the May.

for Ashley Grote and The St Cecilia Singers on the occasion of their 60th anniversary

Let the earth acclaim him

Timothy Dudley-Smith
(b. 1926)

BOB CHILCOTT

Music © Oxford University Press 2009. Text © Timothy Dudley-Smith in Europe and Africa; © Hope Publishing Company in the United States of America and the rest of the world. Reproduced by permission of Oxford University Press.
All rights reserved. Photocopying this copyright material is ILLEGAL.

23
fill his courts with praise. Come in faith, se - cur - ing
In faith, come in faith se -
27
ev - er - last - ing bless - ing: loved by love en - dur - ing
- cur - ing ev - er - last - ing bless - ing:
31
ff
to e - ter - nal days. Let the earth ac - claim him,
ff
to e - ter - nal days. Let the earth ac - claim him,
35
serve the Lord with glad - ness; wor - ship him, and name him
1.
2.
molto rit.
fff
39
source of all our song. song, our song.
fff

to Neil and Kristen on the occasion of their marriage, 5 May 2007

The Lord's my Shepherd

Psalm 23
The Scottish Psalter, 1650

BOB CHILCOTT

First published in Bullard (ed.), *The Oxford Book of Flexible Anthems* (ISBN 978–0–19–335895–9) in an arrangement for unison voices, SA, or SA Men.

© Oxford University Press 2007 and 2009. Photocopying this copyright material is ILLEGAL.

14
S.
A.
T.
B.
p
by.
My
p
p
p
18
soul he doth re - store a - gain; And me to walk doth make With-
22
mp
- in the paths of right-eous-ness, E'en for his own name's sake, e'en
mp
mp

26
for his own name's sake.
unis. mf
Yea,
cresc.
30
S.
mf
Yea, though I walk through death's dark
A.
mf
Yea, though I walk, I walk, will I
T.
B.
though I walk through death's dark vale, Yet will I fear no
mf

33
vale, Yet will I fear, yet will I
fear no ill: For thou art with me, thy rod And
ill: For thou art with me and thy rod And staff me com - fort
37
S.
fear no ill: My ta-ble thou hast fur-nish-ed In pres-ence of my
A.
staff me com - fort still, My ta-ble thou hast fur - nish -
T.
mf
still. My ta - ble thou hast fur - nish -
B.
still. My ta-ble thou hast fur - nish -

41
foes; My head thou dost with oil a-noint, And my cup o - ver -
- ed, And my cup o - ver -
- ed, My head thou dost a - noint, And my
- ed, My head thou dost a - noint, And my
45
f
- flows, o - ver - flows.
f
- flows, my cup o - ver - flows.
f
cup o - ver - flows.
f
cup o - ver - flows.
f
mp
(Man.)

51
DESCANT mf
Good-ness and mer-cy all my life Shall sure-ly
S.
A.
mf
Good-ness and mer - cy all my life Shall sure-ly fol - low
T.
B.
mf
mf
(Ped.)
56
f
fol - low me: And in my Fa - ther's heart al - way My
f
me: And in my Fa - ther's heart al-way My dwell-ing-place shall
f
f

60
mp
dwell-ing-place shall be, shall be,
mp
be, my dwell-ing-place shall be,
mp
mp
65
p
rit.
my dwell-ing place shall be.
p
my dwell-ing place shall be.
p
rit.
p
(Man.)
(Ped.)

for Becky

The Lord's Prayer

BOB CHILCOTT

© Oxford University Press 2009. Photocopying this copyright material is ILLEGAL.

13
us this day our dai - ly bread; And for-
17
- give us our tres-pas-ses, As we for-give them that tres - pass a -
20
mp cresc.
- gainst us; And lead us not in - to temp - ta - tion, But de - li - ver us from
B. mp cresc.
mp cresc.

24
e - vil.
cresc.
f ma dolce
e - vil, from e - vil. For thine is the king - dom, the
cresc.
f ma dolce
cresc.
f ma dolce
28
glo - ry,
mf dim.
pow - er and the glo - ry, the glo - ry, For ev - er and
glo - ry,
mf dim.
mf dim.
32
p
ev - er, A - men.
p
p dolce

36
mp
Our Fa - ther, Hal-lowed be thy
unis. mp
Our Fa - ther, which art in hea - ven, Hal-lowed be thy
mp
40
Name, Thy king - dom come, Thy will be done, as it is in
Name, Thy king - dom come, Thy will be done, in earth as it is in
44
hea - ven.
Give us
cresc.
hea - ven, in hea - ven. Give us this day our dai - ly
cresc.
hea - ven. Give us this day our dai - ly
cresc.

48
bread; And for - give us, As them that
bread; And for - give us our tres-pas-ses As we for-give them that
51
mf
tres - pass a - gainst us; And lead us not in - to temp - ta - tion, But de-
T.
B. mf
mf
55
e - vil.
cresc.
f ma dolce
- li - ver us from e - vil, from e - vil. For thine is the
cresc.
f ma dolce
cresc.
f ma dolce

59
glo - ry,
mf dim.
king - dom, the pow - er and the glo - ry, the glo - ry, For
glo - ry,
mf dim.
mf dim.
63
p dolce
ev - er and ev - er, A - men,
ev - er, for ev - er,
p dolce
p dolce
67
rit.
a - men, a - men.
rit.

for the Crescent City Choral Festival, New Orleans, and Cheryl Dupont, Director

This day

Jewish text
adap. Bob Chilcott

BOB CHILCOTT

An accompaniment for strings and harp is available to hire from the publisher's Hire Library or appropriate agent.

First published as part of the larger work, *This Day* (ISBN 978–0–19–335933–8), scored for SA and piano.

© Oxford University Press 2007 and 2009. Photocopying this copyright material is ILLEGAL.

7
mf
This day in-scribe us for a hap-py, hap-py life.
mf
mf
10
mp
mf
S.
This day hear our cry.
This day ac-cept our prayer in
mp
mf
A.
This day hear our cry.
This day ac-
mp
mf
T.
This day hear our cry.
This day ac-
mp
mf
B.
This day hear our cry.
This day, this
mp
mf

13
mer - cy and fa-vour, This day sup-port us with your right - eous hand.
- cept our prayer with fa - vour, and with your right - eous hand.
- cept our prayer with fa - vour, with your right - eous hand.
day, this day, This day, with your right - eous hand.
16
f
This day ac-cept our prayer in mer - cy and fa-vour, This day, this
mf dim.
This day, this day, This day, this
This day, this day, This day, this
This day, this day, This day, this

19
mp
day.
dolce
This day, this
mp
day.
dolce
This day will you strength us.
mp
day.
dolce
This day will you strength us.
mp
day.
dolce
This day will you strength us.
mp dolce
22
day.
This day, this day.
This day will you bless us.
This day will you lift us,
vi - sit us for good.
This day will you bless us.
This day will you lift us,
vi - sit us for good.
This day will you bless us.
This day will you lift us,
vi - sit us for good.

25
mf
This day in-scribe us for a hap-py, hap-py life.
This day in-scribe us for a hap-py, hap-py life.
This day in-scribe us for a hap-py, hap-py life.
This day in-scribe us for a hap-py, hap-py life.
28
mp
poco rit.
a tempo
espress.
This day hear our cry. A - men,
This day hear our cry. A - men, a -
This day hear our cry. A - - -
This day hear our cry. A - men,

31
mf
a - men, a - men, a - men, a -
mf
- men, a - men, a - - men, a -
mf
- men, a - men, a - men, a -
mf
a - - men, a - men, a - men, a -
mf
35
dim.
p
poco rit.
a bit slower
rit.
- men, a - men.
dim.
p
- men, a - men.
dim.
p
- men, a - men.
dim.
p
- men, a - men.
poco rit.
a bit slower
rit.
dim.
p